SONGS
OF
INNOCENCE

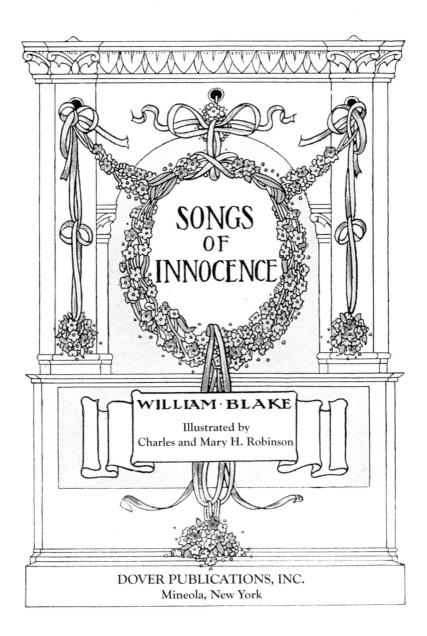

SONGS
OF
INNOCENCE

WILLIAM·BLAKE

Illustrated by
Charles and Mary H. Robinson

DOVER PUBLICATIONS, INC.
Mineola, New York

Bibliographical Note

Songs of Innocence, first published by Dover Publications, Inc., in 2011, is an unabridged republication of the work originally published by J. M. Dent & Sons, London, and E. P. Dutton & Company, New York, in 1912.

Library of Congress Cataloging-in-Publication Data

Blake, William, 1757–1827.
    Songs of innocence / William Blake ; illustrated by Charles and Mary H. Robinson.
        p. cm.
    ISBN-13: 978-0-486-47604-9
    ISBN-10: 0-486-47604-9
    I. Robinson, Charles. II. Robinson, Mary H. III. Title.

PR4144.S6 2011
821'.7—dc22

                                                            20100470366

Manufactured in the United States by Courier Corporation
47604901
www.doverpublications.com

CONTENTS

SONGS OF INNOCENCE

SONGS OF INNOCENCE

SOME POEMS FROM SONGS OF EXPERIENCE

LIST OF

COLOURED ILLUSTRATIONS

SONGS
OF
INNOCENCE

On a cloud I saw a child.

INTRODUCTION

PIPING down the valleys wild,
Piping songs of pleasant glee,
On a cloud I saw a child,
And he laughing said to me:—

" Pipe a song about a lamb ":
So I piped with merry cheer.
" Piper, pipe that song again ":
So I piped; he wept to hear.

" Drop thy pipe, thy happy pipe,
Sing thy songs of happy cheer ":
So I sung the same again,
While he wept with joy to hear.

" Piper, sit thee down and write
In a book that all may read "—
So he vanish'd from my sight;
And I pluck'd a hollow reed,

And I made a rural pen,
And I stain'd the water clear,
And I wrote my happy songs
Every child may joy to hear.

THE SHEPHERD

How sweet is the shepherd's sweet lot;
From the morn to the evening he strays;
He shall follow his sheep all the day,
And his tongue shall be filled with praise.

For he hears the lambs' innocent call,
And he hears the ewes' tender reply;
He is watchful while they are in peace,
For they know when their shepherd is nigh.

THE ECHOING GREEN

THE sun does arise
And make happy the skies;
The merry bells ring
To welcome the spring;
The skylark and thrush,
The birds of the bush,
Sing louder around
To the bells' cheerful sound,
While our sports shall be seen
On the echoing green.

Old John with white hair
Does laugh away care,
Sitting under the oak
Among the old folk.
They laugh at our play,
And soon they all say :
" Such, such were the joys
When we, all girls and boys,

THE ECHOING GREEN

In our youth-time were seen
On the echoing green."

Till the little ones, weary,
No more can be merry;
The sun does descend,
And our sports have an end.
Round the laps of their mothers
Many sisters and brothers,
Like birds in their nest,
Are ready for rest;
And sport no more seen
On the darkening green.

THE LAMB

LITTLE lamb, who made thee?
Dost thou know who made thee,
Gave thee life and bid thee feed
By the stream and o'er the mead;
Gave thee clothing of delight,
Softest clothing, woolly, bright;
Gave thee such a tender voice
Making all the vales rejoice;
    Little lamb, who made thee?
    Dost thou know who made thee?

Little lamb, I'll tell thee,
Little lamb, I'll tell thee.
He is called by thy name,
For he calls himself a Lamb:

Little Lamb, who made thee ?

THE LAMB

He is meek and he is mild,
He became a little child.
I a child and thou a lamb,
We are called by his name.
    Little lamb, God bless thee,
    Little lamb, God bless thee.

THE LITTLE BLACK BOY

My mother bore me in the southern wild,
And I am black, but oh! my soul is white;
White as an angel is the English child,
But I am black, as if bereaved of light.

My mother taught me underneath a tree,
And sitting down before the heat of day,
She took me on her lap, and kissed me,
And, pointing to the east, began to say:—

" Look on the rising sun,—there God does live,
And gives his light, and gives his heat away;
And flowers, and trees, and beast, and men receive
Comfort in morning, joy in the noon-day.

" And we are put on earth a little space,
That we may learn to bear the beams of love;
And these black bodies and this sun–burnt face
Are but a cloud, and like a shady grove.

" For when our souls have learnt the heat to bear,
The clouds will vanish, we shall hear his voice,
Saying, ' Come out from the grove, my love and
     care,
And round my golden tent like lambs rejoice.' "

Thus did my mother say, and kissed me;
And thus l say to little English boy,—
" When I from black, and he from white cloud
     free,
And round the tent of God like lambs we joy,

" I'll shade him from the heat, till he can bear
To lean in joy upon our Father's knee;
And then I'll stand, and stroke his silver hair,
And be like him, and he will then love me."

THE BLOSSOM

MERRY, merry sparrow,
Under leaves so green,
    A happy blossom
Sees you, swift as arrow,
Seek your cradle narrow
    Near my bosom.

Pretty, pretty robin,
Under leaves so green,
    A happy blossom
Hears you sobbing, sobbing,
Pretty, pretty robin,
    Near my bosom.

THE CHIMNEY-SWEEPER

WHEN my mother died I was very young,
And my father sold me while yet my tongue
Could scarcely cry "'weep, 'weep, 'weep, 'weep!"
So your chimneys I sweep and in soot I sleep.

There's little Tom Dacre, who cried when his
   head,
That curl'd like a lamb's back, was shaved: so
   I said:
"Hush, Tom, never mind it, for when your head's
   bare
You know that the soot cannot spoil your white
   hair."

And so he was quiet; and that very night,
As Tom was a-sleeping, he had such a sight;
That thousands of sweepers, Dick, Joe, Ned, and
    Jack,
Were all of them lock'd up in coffins of black.

And by came an angel who had a bright key,
And he open'd the coffins and set them all free;
Then down a green plain, leaping, laughing they
    run,
And wash in a river and shine in the sun.

Then naked and white, all their bags left behind,
They rise upon clouds and sport in the wind;
And the angel told Tom if he'd be a good boy,
He'd have God for his father and never want joy.

And so Tom awoke; and we rose in the dark,
And got with our bags and our brushes to work.
Though the morning was cold Tom was happy
    and warm:
So if all do their duty they need not fear harm.

THE LITTLE BOY LOST

FATHER! father! where are you going?
  Oh, do not walk so fast.
Speak, father, speak to your little boy,
  Or else I shall be lost.

The night was dark, no father was there;
  The child was wet with dew;
The mire was deep and the child did weep,
  And away the vapour flew.

THE
LITTLE BOY FOUND

THE little boy lost in the lonely fen,
   Led by the wandering light,
Began to cry; but God, ever nigh,
   Appear'd like his father in white;

He kiss'd the child, and by the hand led,
   And to his mother brought,
Who, in sorrow pale, thro' the lonely dale,
   Her little boy weeping sought.

A CRADLE SONG

SWEET dreams, form a shade
O'er my lovely infant's head;
Sweet dreams of pleasant streams
By happy, silent, moony beams.

Sweet sleep, with soft down
Weave thy brows an infant crown.
Sweet sleep, angel mild,
Hover o'er my happy child.

Sweet smiles in the night
Hover over my delight;
Sweet smiles, mother's smiles,
All the livelong night beguiles.

Sweet moans, dove-like sighs,
Chase not slumber from thy eyes.
Sweet moans, sweeter smiles,
All the dove-like moans beguiles.

Sleep, sleep, happy child,
All creation slept and smiled ;
Sleep, sleep, happy sleep,
While o'er thee thy mother weep.

Sweet babe, in thy face
Holy image I can trace.
Sweet babe, once like thee
Thy Maker lay and wept for me.

Wept for me, for thee, for all
When he was an infant small.
Thou his image ever see,
Heavenly face that smiles on thee.

Smiles on thee, on me, on all ;
Who became an infant small.
Infant smiles are his own smiles ;
Heaven and earth to peace beguiles.

THE DIVINE IMAGE

To mercy, pity, peace, and love
  All pray in their distress;
And to these virtues of delight
  Return their thankfulness.

For mercy, pity, peace, and love
  Is God, our Father dear;
And mercy, pity, peace, and love
  Is man His child and care.

For mercy has a human heart,
  Pity a human face;
And love, the human form divine,
  And peace, the human dress.

Then every man of every clime
  That prays in his distress,
Prays to the human form divine,
  Love, Mercy, Pity, Peace.

And all must love the human form
In heathen, Turk, or Jew ;
Where mercy, love, and pity dwell,
There God is dwelling too.

HOLY THURSDAY

'Twas on a Holy Thursday, their innocent faces
    clean,
The children walking two and two, in red and
    blue and green,
Grey-headed beadles walk'd before, with wands
    as white as snow,
Till into the high dome of Paul's they like
    Thames' waters flow.

O what a multitude they seem'd, these flowers of
    London town;

Seated in companies, they sit with radiance all
    their own.
The hum of multitudes was there, but multitudes
    of lambs,
Thousands of little boys and girls raising their
    innocent hands.

Now like a mighty wind they raise to heaven the
    voice of song,
Or like harmonious thunderings the seats of
    heaven among.
Beneath them sit the aged men, wise guardians of
    the poor;
Then cherish pity, lest you drive an angel from
    your door.

NIGHT

THE sun descending in the west,
The evening star does shine ;
The birds are silent in their nest,
And I must seek for mine.
The moon, like a flower,
In heaven's high bower,
With silent delight
Sits and smiles on the night.

Farewell, green fields and happy groves,
Where flocks have took delight ;
Where lambs have nibbled, silent moves
The feet of angels bright.
Unseen they pour blessing,
And joy without ceasing,
On each bud and blossom
And each sleeping bosom.

They look in every thoughtless nest,
Where birds are cover'd warm;
They visit caves of every beast,
To keep them all from harm.
If they see any weeping
That should have been sleeping,
They pour sleep on their head,
And sit down by their bed.

When wolves and tigers howl for prey
They pitying stand and weep,
Seeking to drive their thirst away,
And keep them from the sheep.
But if they rush dreadful,
The angels most heedful
Receive each mild spirit,
New worlds to inherit.

And there the lion's ruddy eyes
Shall flow with tears of gold,
And pitying the tender cries,
And walking round the fold,

"And I must seek for mine."

Saying, " Wrath, by his meekness
And by his health, sickness
Is driven away
From our immortal day.

" And now beside thee, bleating lamb,
I can lie down and sleep;
Or think on him who bore thy name,
Graze after thee, and weep.
For, wash'd in life's river,
My bright mane for ever
Shall shine like the gold
As I guard o'er the fold."

SPRING

Sound the flute!
Now it's mute.
Birds delight
Day and night;
Nightingale
In the dale,
Lark in sky,
Merrily,
Merrily, merrily, to welcome in the year

Little boy,
Full of joy;
Little girl,
Sweet and small;
Cock does crow,
So do you.
Merry voice,
Infant noise,
Merrily, merrily, to welcome in the year.

Little lamb,
Here I am;
Come and lick
My white neck;
Let me pull
Your soft wool;
Let me kiss
Your soft face:
Merrily, merrily, we welcome in the year.

NURSE'S SONG

WHEN the voices of children are heard on the
    green
And laughing is heard on the hill,
My heart is at rest within my breast,
And everything else is still.

Then come home, my children, the sun is gone
    down,
And the dews of night arise;
Come, come, leave off play, and let us away
Till the morning appears in the skies.

No, no, let us play, for it is yet day,
And we cannot go to sleep;
Besides in the sky the little birds fly,
And the hills are all cover'd with sheep.

Well, well, go and play till the light fades away,
And then go home to bed.
The little ones leap'd and shouted and laugh'd
And all the hills echoed.

INFANT
JOY

I HAVE no name,
I am but two days old.
What shall I call thee?
I happy am,
Joy is my name.—
Sweet joy befall thee!

Pretty joy!
Sweet joy but two days old.
Sweet joy I call thee.
Thou dost smile,
I sing the while,
Sweet joy befall thee!

A DREAM

ONCE a dream did weave a shade
O'er my angel-guarded bed,
That an emmet lost its way
Where on grass methought I lay.

Troubled, wilder'd, and forlorn,
Dark, benighted, travel, travel-worn,
Over many a tangled spray,
All heart-broke I heard her say :

"O my children ! do they cry ?
Do they hear their father sigh ?
Now they look abroad to see,
Now return and weep for me."

Pitying I dropp'd a tear;
But I saw a glow-worm near:
Who replied, " What wailing wight
Calls the watchman of the night?

" I am set to light the ground
While the beetle goes his round:
Follow now the beetle's hum;
Little wanderer, hie thee home."

That an Emmet lost its way.

LAUGHING SONG

WHEN the green woods laugh with the voice of
    joy,
And the dimpling stream runs laughing by,
When the air does laugh with our merry wit,
And the green hill laughs with the noise of it;

When the meadows laugh with lively green,
And the grasshopper laughs in the merry scene,
When Mary and Susan and Emily
With their sweet round mouths sing Ha, ha, he!

When the painted birds laugh in the shade,
When our table with cherries and nuts is spread,
Come live and be happy and join with me
To sing the sweet chorus of Ha, ha, he!

THE SCHOOL-BOY

I LOVE to rise in a summer morn
    When the birds sing on every tree;
The distant huntsman winds his horn,
    And the sky-lark sings with me.
    O! what sweet company.

But to go to school in a summer morn,
    O! it drives all joy away;
Under a cruel eye outworn,
    The little ones spend the day
    In sighing and dismay.

Ah! then at times I drooping sit,
    And spend many an anxious hour;
Nor in my book can I take delight
    Nor sit in learning's bower,
    Worn thro' with the dreary shower.

How can the bird, that is born for joy,
  Sit in a cage and sing?
How can a child, when fears annoy,
  But droop his tender wing,
  And forget his youthful spring?

O father and mother, if buds are nipp'd,
  And blossoms blown away,
And if the tender plants are stripp'd
  Of their joy in the springing day,
  By sorrow and care's dismay,

How shall the summer arise in joy,
  Or the summer fruits appear?
Or how shall we gather what griefs destroy,
  Or bless the mellowing year,
  When the blasts of winter appear?

ON ANOTHER'S SORROW

Can I see another's woe,
And not be in sorrow too?
Can I see another's grief,
And not seek for kind relief?

Can I see a falling tear,
And not feel my sorrow's share?
Can a father see his child
Weep, nor be with sorrow fill'd?

Can a mother sit and hear
An infant groan, an infant fear?
No, no, never can it be,
Never, never can it be.

And can he who smiles on all
Hear the wren with sorrows small,
Hear the small bird's grief and care,
Hear the woes that infants bear,

And not sit beside the nest,
Pouring pity in their breast;
And not sit the cradle near,
Weeping tear on infant's tear;

And not sit both night and day,
Wiping all our tears away?
O! no, never can it be,
Never, never can it be.

He doth give his joy to all;
He becomes an infant small;
He becomes a man of woe;
He doth feel the sorrow too.

Think not thou canst sigh a sigh
And thy Maker is not by;
Think not thou canst weep a tear
And thy Maker is not near.

O! he gives to us his joy
That our grief he may destroy:
Till our grief is fled and gone
He doth sit by us and moan.

THE VOICE OF THE ANCIENT BARD

YOUTH of delight, come hither,
  And see the opening morn,
  Image of truth new-born.
Doubt is fled and clouds of reason,
Dark disputes and artful teasing.
  Folly is an endless maze,
  Tangled roots perplex her ways,
  How many have fallen there !
They stumble all night over bones of the dead,
And feel they know not what but care,
And wish to lead others when they should be led.

SOME POEMS

FROM

SONGS OF EXPERIENCE

MY
PRETTY ROSE TREE

A FLOWER was offer'd to me,
Such a flower as May never bore;
But I said, I've a pretty rose-tree,
And I pass'd the sweet flower o'er.

Then I went to my pretty rose-tree,
To tend her by day and by night;
But my rose turn'd away with jealousy,
And her thorns were my only delight.

THE LILY

THE modest rose puts forth a thorn,
The humble sheep a threatening horn ;
  While the lily white shall in love delight,
Nor a thorn nor a threat stain her beauty bright.

The Lily white.

THE SICK ROSE

O ROSE, thou art sick:
The invisible worm,
That flies in the night
In the howling storm,

Has found out thy bed
Of crimson joy;
And his dark secret love
Does thy life destroy.

THE FLY

LITTLE fly,
Thy summer's play
My thoughtless hand
Has brush'd away.

Am not I
A fly like thee?
Or art not thou
A man like me?

For I dance,
And drink, and sing,
Till some blind hand
Shall brush my wing.

If thought is life
And strength and breath,
And the want
Of thought is death;

Then am I
A happy fly,
If I live
Or if I die.

THE TIGER

TIGER, tiger, burning bright
In the forests of the night,
What immortal hand or eye
Could frame thy fearful symmetry?

In what distant deeps or skies
Burnt the fire of thine eyes?
On what wings dare he aspire?
What the hand dare seize the fire?

And what shoulder, and what art,
Could twist the sinews of thy heart?
And when thy heart began to beat,
What dread hand? and what dread feet?

What the hammer? what the chain?
In what furnace was thy brain?
What the anvil? what dread grasp
Dare its deadly terrors clasp?

Tiger, Tiger, burning bright.

When the stars threw down their spears,
And water'd heaven with their tears,
Did he smile his work to see?
Did he who made the lamb make thee?

Tiger, tiger, burning bright
In the forests of the night,
What immortal hand or eye
Dare frame thy fearful symmetry?

THE ANGEL

I DREAMT a dream! what can it mean?
And that I was a maiden queen,
Guarded by an angel mild:
Witless woe was ne'er beguiled.

And I wept both night and day,
And he wiped my tears away,
And I wept both day and night,
And hid from him my heart's delight.

So he took his wings and fled;
Then the morn blush'd rosy red;
I dried my tears and arm'd my fears
With ten thousand shields and spears.

Soon my angel came again:
I was arm'd, he came in vain;
For the time of youth was fled,
And grey hairs were on my head.

THE LITTLE GIRL LOST

IN futurity
I prophetic see
That the earth from sleep
(Grave the sentence deep)

Shall arise and seek
For her maker meek ;
And the desert wild
Become a garden mild.

In the southern clime,
Where the summer's prime
Never fades away,
Lovely Lyca lay.

Seven summers old
Lovely Lyca told;
She had wander'd long
Hearing wild birds' song.

Sweet sleep, come to me
Underneath this tree.
Do father, mother weep?
Where can Lyca sleep?

Lost in the desert wild
Is your little child.
How can Lyca sleep
If her mother weep?

If her heart does ache,
Then let Lyca wake;
If my mother sleep,
Lyca shall not weep.

Frowning, frowning night,
O'er this desert bright,
Let thy moon arise
While I close my eyes.

Sleeping Lyca lay:
While the beasts of prey,
Come from caverns deep,
View'd the maid asleep.

The kingly lion stood,
And the virgin view'd,
Then he gamboll'd round
O'er the hallow'd ground.

Leopards, tigers play
Round her as she lay,
While the lion old
Bow'd his mane of gold,

And her bosom lick,
And upon her neck
From his eyes of flame
Ruby tears there came.

While the lioness
Loosed her slender dress,
And naked they convey'd
To caves the sleeping maid.

THE
LITTLE GIRL FOUND

ALL the night in woe
Lyca's parents go
Over valleys deep,
While the deserts weep.

Tired and woe-begone,
Hoarse with making moan,
Arm in arm seven days
They traced the desert ways.

Seven nights they sleep
Among shadows deep,
And dreamed they see their child
Starved in desert wild.

Pale, through pathless ways
The fancied image strays,
Famish'd, weeping, weak,
With hollow piteous shriek.

Rising from unrest
The trembling woman press'd
With feet of weary woe:
She could no further go.

In his arms he bore
Her, arm'd with sorrow sore;
Till before their way
A couching lion lay.

Turning back was vain:
Soon his heavy mane
Bore them to the ground;
Then he stalk'd around,

Smelling to his prey;
But their fears allay
When he licks their hands,
And silent by them stands.

They look upon his eyes
Fill'd with deep surprise;
And, wondering, behold
A spirit arm'd in gold—

On his head a crown;
On his shoulders down
Flow'd his golden hair;
Gone was all their care.

" Follow me," he said;
" Weep not for the maid;
" In my palace deep
" Lyca lies asleep."

Then they followed
Where the vision led;
And saw their sleeping child
Among tigers wild.

To this day they dwell
In a lonely dell;
Nor fear the wolvish howl,
Nor the lion's growl.

A LITTLE GIRL LOST

Children of the future age,
Reading this indignant page,
Know that in a former time,
Love, sweet love, was thought a crime!

In the Age of Gold,
Free from winter's cold,
Youth and maiden bright,
To the holy light,
Naked in the sunny beams delight.

Once a youthful pair,
Fill'd with softest care,
Met in garden bright,
Where the holy light
Had just removed the curtains of the night.

65

There in rising day,
On the grass they play;
Parents were afar,
Strangers came not near;
And the maiden soon forgot her fear.

Tired with kisses sweet,
They agree to meet
When the silent sleep
Waves o'er heaven's deep,
And the weary tired wanderers weep.

To her father white
Came the maiden bright;
But his loving look,
Like the holy book,
All her tender limbs with terror shook.

Ona, pale and weak,
To thy father speak!
O the trembling fear,
O the dismal care
That shakes the blossoms of my hoary hair!